Flamingos

Quinn M. Arnold

CREATIVE EDUCATION • CREATIVE PAPERBACKS

seedlings

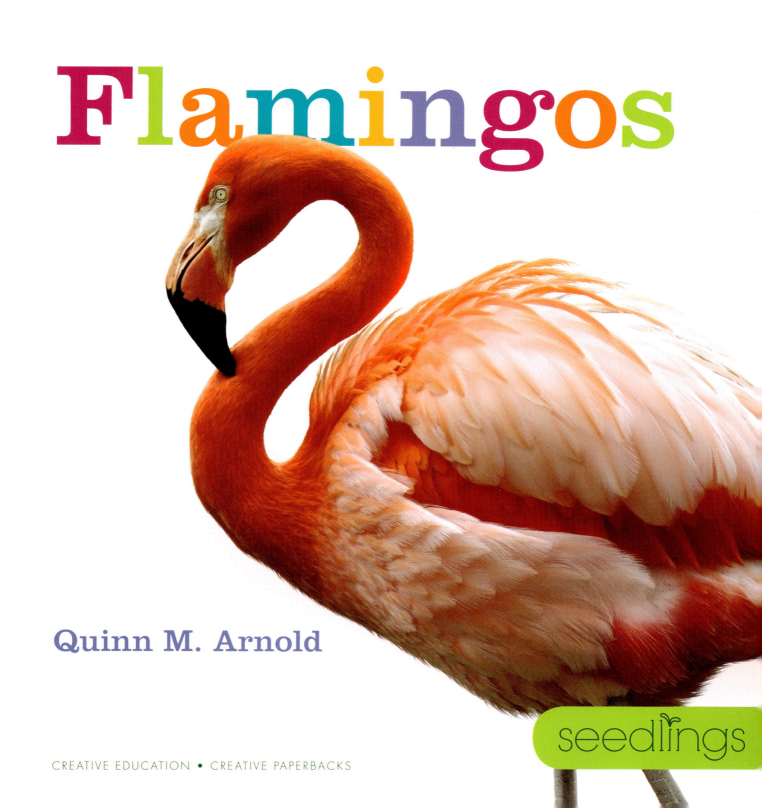

Published by Creative Education and Creative Paperbacks
P.O. Box 227, Mankato, Minnesota 56002
Creative Education and Creative Paperbacks
are imprints of The Creative Company
www.thecreativecompany.us

Design by Ellen Huber; production by Joe Kahnke
Art direction by Rita Marshall
Printed in China

Photographs by Alamy (epa european pressphoto agency b.v.),
Getty Images (Nikki O'Keefe Images), iStockphoto (jamcgraw,
Roberto_Marcon, mjf99), Minden Pictures (Bill Coster, Elliott
Neep), National Geographic Creative (JOEL SARTORE/NATIONAL
GEOGRAPHIC PHOTO ARK), Shutterstock (cyo bo, Sebastien
Burel, Le Do, Svetlana Foote, Christian Musat, Anna Om,
Roby1960, Auttapol Sangsub, topseller, worldswildlifewonders),
SuperStock (Roger Eritja/age fotostock, NHPA/NHPA)

Copyright © 2018 Creative Education, Creative Paperbacks
International copyright reserved in all countries. No part of
this book may be reproduced in any form without written
permission from the publisher.

Library of Congress Cataloging-in-Publication Data
Names: Arnold, Quinn M., author.
Title: Flamingos / Quinn M. Arnold.
Series: Seedlings.
Includes index.
Summary: A kindergarten-level introduction to flamingos,
covering their growth process, behaviors, the lakes they call
home, and such defining features as their long legs.
Identifiers: LCCN 2016054472 / ISBN 978-1-60818-867-3
(hardcover) / ISBN 978-1-62832-482-2 (pbk) / ISBN 978-1-
56660-915-9 (eBook)

Subjects: LCSH: Flamingos—Juvenile literature.
Classification: LCC QL696.C56 A78 2017 / DDC 598.3/5—dc23

CCSS: RI.K.1, 2, 3, 4, 5, 6, 7;
RI.1.1, 2, 3, 4, 5, 6, 7; RF.K.1, 3; RF.1.1

First Edition HC 9 8 7 6 5 4 3 2 1
First Edition PBK 9 8 7 6 5 4 3 2 1

TABLE OF CONTENTS

Hello, Flamingos! 4

Long-legged Birds 6

Pretty in Pink 8

Bent Bills 10

Time to Eat! 12

Flamingo Chicks 14

What Do Flamingos Do? 16

Goodbye, Flamingos! 18

Picture a Flamingo 20

Words to Know 22

Read More 23

Websites 23

Index 24

Hello, flamingos!

Flamingos are tall birds. They live by warm, salty water.

They form big flocks.

Most flamingos are pink. They can be orange or red, too. Flamingo wings have black feathers.

Flamingos have long necks. Their bills are bent.

They stand on one thin leg to rest.

A flamingo turns its head upside down to eat.

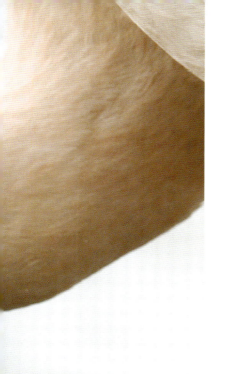

It swings its bill back and forth.
It catches shrimp.
It eats algae, too.

A chick is a baby flamingo. It comes out of an egg.

The chick is gray and fluffy. Its parents take care of it.

Flamingos run across water.

They flap their wings and fly into the air.

Picture a Flamingo

feathers

neck

legs

20

Words to Know

algae: groups of plants that do not have leaves or stems and grow in water

bills: beaks, or parts of birds' faces that stick out

feathers: parts of a bird's body that grow out of its skin

flocks: large groups of birds that live together

Read More

Gibbs, Maddie. *Flamingos.*
New York: PowerKids Press, 2011.

Riggs, Kate. *Flamingos.*
Mankato, Minn.: Creative Education, 2015.

Websites

All Things Animal TV: Flamingos
https://www.youtube.com/watch?v=Pz3XiJac57w
Watch a video to learn more about flamingos.

Super Coloring: Flamingos Coloring Pages
http://www.supercoloring.com/coloring-pages
/birds/flamingos
Print off pictures of flamingos to color.

Note: Every effort has been made to ensure that the websites listed above are suitable for children, that they have educational value, and that they contain no inappropriate material. However, because of the nature of the Internet, it is impossible to guarantee that these sites will remain active indefinitely or that their contents will not be altered.

Index

bills 10, 13
chicks 14, 15
colors 8, 15
eggs 14
feathers 8
flocks 7
food 12, 13
legs 11
necks 10
water 6, 16
wings 8, 17